NORT

Ghos

C000006795

Prepare to be frightened by these terrifying
tales from around North Wales

By

Richard Holland

BRADWELL
BOOKS

Published by Bradwell Books
9 Orgreave Close Sheffield S13 9NP
Email: books@bradwellbooks.co.uk

British Library Cataloguing in Publication Data: a catalogue
record for this book is available from the British Library.

1st Edition
ISBN: 9781902674445

Print: Gomer Press, Llandysul, Ceredigion SA44 4JL

Design by: JenksDesign
Photograph Credits

CONTENTS

Plas Mawr in Conwy is one of the many historic haunted houses which can be visited in North Wales

INTRODUCTION

I have lived in North Wales for nearly forty years and have been writing about its ghosts and folklore for twenty-five of them. My fascination remains undimmed. Surely, for such a small country with a comparatively low population, Wales must be the most haunted country in the world?

The ghosts of North Wales are as wild and as fascinating as the land they haunt. Here can be found the ghosts of profligate squires, cruel murderers and fierce knights, weird animal-like apparitions and grotesque half-human creatures. There are many gentler ghosts, too, including unearthly music emanating from old churches, and the quiet presence of former occupants of homes they loved and apparently cannot bear to leave. Some of these ghosts are of great antiquity: one indeed may date back more than three thousand years to the Bronze Age.

Many of the region's most interesting and historic houses are haunted and you will find plenty of other places worth visiting for more than just their spooky reputations. You will also be lucky enough to pass through some of the UK's most beautiful and spectacular scenery while travelling to and from them.

Naturally, a book of this type can only hint at the very many ghost stories and haunted sites in North Wales. For a much fuller review of the haunted heritage of Wales, you might like to read my *Haunted Wales: A Guide to Welsh Ghostlore* published in 2011. I would also be pleased to welcome you over at my website devoted to ghosts and folklore in Britain, www.uncannyuk.com.

THE TREASURE GUARDIAN

Perhaps the most celebrated ghost story of all from Wales is the one surrounding the finding of the Golden Cape, a fascinating artefact of worked gold dating from the Bronze Age. The incidents all took place about a hundred yards away from where I was brought up in my home town of Mold (Yr Wyddgrug). Long before the modern housing estate I lived on was built the area was called by some Bryn yr Ellyllon, or 'Goblin Hill'. It was a partly wooded, unpopulated hill on the eastern outskirts of Mold and had a spooky reputation thanks to a ghost known by the name of Brenin yr Allt, which translates as 'King of the Hill'.

A replica of the Mold Gold Cape, in the care of the Flintshire Library Service.
The cape was discovered in a Bronze Age burial mound which had previously been
haunted, some said by a figure in 'golden armour'. © Richard Holland

The Brenin yr Allt haunted the 'Tomen', a mound beside the road, a place that tended to be avoided after dark. There are two accounts dating from the early 19th century of encounters with the ghost. In 1810 or thereabouts a woman had been forced to go out late at night in search of her drunken husband. She found him, and was leading him back home, when both of them saw the Brenin yr Allt standing on the mound. This 'scared the woman into fits and the man into sobriety'. In 1828 another woman had seen the ghost and the sight of it sent her mad.

Two years later we come to the most famous sighting. A farmwife was returning late from market when she noticed an odd glow emanating from the woods near the summit of Bryn yr Ellyllon. Suddenly a huge figure clad in gold emerged from the woods, strode boldly across the lane and vanished into the mound. Startled, the woman immediately turned her horse around and went and told the vicar what had happened.

In 1833, after three thousand years or so, the Tomen was finally disturbed. Noticing it was composed of small stones, a Mr Langford, who rented the field on which it stood, ordered that it be dug up and the stones used to fill in a hole by the side of the road. Destroying what we now know to have been a prehistoric cairn, the labourers found within it the remains of a Bronze Age burial which included hundreds of amber beads and a sheet of gold. The latter is now known as the Gold Cape. Finely worked to reproduce woven patterns, it is a unique garment which would probably have fitted over the shoulders (front and back) of a very important person. Initially it was dumped in a wheelbarrow but when somebody realised it was made of gold, numerous chunks were ripped from it. Now on proud display in the British Museum, it is sadly only about two-thirds of its original size.

On the face of it, the discovery of this treasure validates the belief in the Brenin yr Allt. In Welsh folklore it was firmly believed that ghosts haunted the location of hidden valuables. Unfortunately, the accounts of the sightings of the spook were all published after the finding of the gold, and there is always the risk that the stories were made up by people after the event. Nevertheless, there is some evidence to suggest there was a genuine belief in a ghost on Bryn yr Ellyllon years before the

Pentre Hill, in Mold, as it is today. The black plaque against the wall was set up in the 1920s to commemorate the finding of the Gold Cape. It's greatly inaccurate, however: it gives the wrong date for the discovery, states that the artefact was intended to be worn by a horse and suggests it may have belonged to Benlli Gawr, a nobleman from the Dark Ages who lived thousands of years after the cape was made. © Richard Holland

discovery. In addition to the hill's suggestive name, Mr Langford is reported to have taken the news to an old woman who lived on the estate because she had seen the ghost many years before.

The memory of a man who had seen the opened cairn and the Gold Cape lying in the wheelbarrow on the day it was found is also useful evidence. Although he was writing sixty-eight years after the event (he had been a boy of thirteen at the time), he clearly remembered that the field in which the Tomen had stood was believed to be haunted. His recollection was that the ghost was supposedly 'a headless warrior riding a grey horse' rather than a man in golden armour, however.

Is the Gold Cape solid gold evidence that ghosts exist? I leave that for the reader to decide.

THE SECRET OF POWIS CASTLE

Powis Castle is a spectacular medieval fortress originally built by a Welsh nobleman in the 13th century. It rises dramatically from a rocky crag near Welshpool (Y Trallwng) in Powys, its distinctively coloured walls of red sandstone dominating the landscape. In addition to the usual complement of fine furniture and art treasures (including a collection rare antiques from India), Powis Castle is particularly famed for its baroque terraced gardens, which have survived virtually intact from the late 17th century. The Castle and grounds are now in the care of the National Trust.

The ghost story of Powis Castle is one of the best known from Wales, since it involved an important family and comes to us

Powis Castle was the scene of one of the best-known ghost stories from Wales, in which a poor woman was shown the hiding place of some important documents by a ghost. © Richard Holland

almost first-hand. It was told by the witness herself to a Methodist preacher and he related it to a Mr Wright, who published it. The events took place in the 18th century. The witness was an elderly lady, a very religious person, who went around the grander homes of that part of old Montgomeryshire with her own little spinning wheel, offering to do any little jobs of weaving that might be required. She would frequently call at Powis Castle. On this occasion, the family was away in London but the steward and his wife agreed to employ her as usual. However, they insisted she stay the night, since, they said, there was more than one day's worth of work to be done. This is where the lady's story becomes spooky.

'When bedtime arrived, two or three servants in company, with each a lighted candle in her hand, conducted her to her lodging. They led her to a ground-floor room, with a boarded floor and two sash windows. The room was grandly furnished, and had a genteel bed in one corner of it. They had made her a good fire, and had placed her chair and table before it, and a large lighted candle upon the table. They told her that was her bedroom, and that she might go to sleep when she pleased. They then wished her a good night and withdrew altogether, pulling the door quickly after them.

'When they were gone, she gazed awhile at the fine furniture, under no small astonishment that they should put such a poor person as her in so grand a room, and bed, with all the apparatus of fire, chair, table and a candle. She was also surprised at the circumstance of the servants coming so many together, with each of them a candle. However, after gazing about her some little time, she sat down and took a small Welsh Bible out of her pocket, which she always carried about with her, and in which she usually read a chapter – chiefly in the New Testament – before she said her prayers and went to bed.

'While she was reading she heard the door open, and turning her head, saw a gentleman enter in a gold-laced hat and waistcoat, and the rest of his dress corresponding therewith. He walked down by the sash window to the corner of the room and then returned. When he came to the first window on his return (the bottom of which was nearly breast high), he rested his elbow on the bottom of the window, and the side of his face upon the palm of the hand, and stood in that leaning position for some time, with his side partly towards her. She looked at him earnestly to see if she knew him, but, though from her frequent intercourse with them, she had a personal knowledge of all the present family, he appeared a stranger to her. She supposed afterwards that he stood in this manner to encourage her to speak; but as she did not, after some little time he walked off, pulling the door after him.

'She began now to be much alarmed, concluding it to be an apparition, and that they had put her there on purpose. This was really the case. The room, it seems, had been disturbed for a long time, so that nobody could sleep peaceably in it, and as she passed for a very serious woman, the servants took it into their heads to put the Methodist and Spirit together, to see what they would make of it. Startled at this thought, she rose from her chair, and kneeled down by the bedside to say her prayers. 'While she was praying he came in again, walked round the room, and came close behind her. She had it on her mind to speak, but when she attempted it she was so very much agitated that she could not utter a word. He walked out of the room again, pulling the door after him as before. She prayed that God would strengthen her and not suffer her to be tried beyond what she could bear. She recovered her spirits, and thought she felt more confidence and resolution, and determined if he came in again she would speak to him.

'He presently came in again, walked around and came behind as before; she turned her head and said, "Pray, sir, who are you and what do you want?" He put up his finger, and said, "Take up the candle and follow me, and I will tell you." She got up, took up the candle, and followed him out of the room. He led her through a long boarded passage till they came to the door of another room, which she opened, and went in. It was a small room, or what might be called a large closet.

"'As the room was small, and I believed him to be a Spirit," she said, "I stopped at the door; he turned and said, 'Walk in, I will not hurt you.' So I walked in. He said, 'Observe what I do.' I said, 'I will.'

"'He stooped, and tore up one of the boards of the floor, and there appeared under it a box with an iron handle in the lid. He said, 'Do you see that box?' I said, 'Yes, I do.' He then stepped to one side of the room, and showed me a crevice in the wall, where he said a key was hid that would open it. He said, 'This box and key must be taken out, and sent to the Earl in London' (naming the Earl, and his place of residence in the city). He said, 'Will you see it done?' I said, 'I will do my best to get it done.' He said, 'Do, and I will trouble the house no more.' He then walked out of the room and left me.

"'I stepped to the room door and set up a shout. The steward and his wife, and the other servants, came to me immediately, all clung together, with a number of lights in their hands. It seems they had all had been waiting to see the issue of the interview betwixt me and the apparition. They asked me what was the matter? I told them the foregoing circumstances, and showed them the box. The steward durst not meddle with it, but his wife had more courage, and with the help of the other servants, lugged it out, and found the key."

'She said by their lifting it, it appeared to be pretty heavy, but that she did not see it opened, and, therefore, did not know what it contained; perhaps money, or writings of consequence to the family, or both. They took it away with them, and she then went to bed and slept peaceably till the morning. It appeared afterwards that they sent the box to the Earl in London, with an account of the manner of its discovery and by whom; and the Earl sent down orders immediately to the steward to inform the poor woman who had been the occasion of this discovery, that if she would come and reside in his family, she would be comfortably provided for, for the remainder of her days; or, if she did not choose to reside constantly with them, if she would let them know when she wanted assistance, she should be liberally supplied at his Lordship's expense as long as he lived. It was a known fact in the neighbourhood that she had been so supplied from his Lordship's family from the time the affair was said to have happened and continued to be so at the time she gave this account.'

THE DRUNKEN GHOST OF PLAS YN RHIW

Another National Trust property – much less grand but no less interesting – is Plas yn Rhiw on the Llŷn Peninsula. The interior of this small manor house which dates back to the Tudor period was left virtually untouched since the 1920s by the elderly ladies who set up home in splendid isolation here. The charming landscaped gardens are well worth a visit too, if only for the spectacular views over the bay known as 'Hell's Mouth' (Pwll y Neigwl).

An interesting first-hand report of a haunting at Plas yn Rhiw was recorded in 1936 in a book called *True Ghost Stories*, compiled by two society ladies, Marchioness Townshend of Raynham and her friend Maude M C ffoulkes. The Hon. Mrs Greville Nugent was later responsible for designing the gardens at Plas yn Rhiw, but at the time of her adventure she was merely a guest in the house, which was then being used as a holiday home and yet to be occupied permanently. She writes:

'In the summer of 1892, I was staying with my friend the late Lady Strickland, at an old manor house called Plas yn Rhiw, near Pwllheli. I was the only visitor, and one night Lady Strickland and I sat up so late playing cards that it was long past midnight when we prepared to go to bed. In view of what happened, I should mention that the servants of Plas yn Rhiw (who had all gone to bed long before) slept in another wing, and as they used the back staircase to go to their rooms, no one but ourselves could possibly be using the front staircase at that hour. 'The old house was in absolute stillness, and the moonlight lay in pools of silver on the oak staircase. My bedroom, on the first floor, faced the landing, and Lady Strickland, who slept on the floor above me, was just in the act of lighting her candle from mine, when we heard heavy footsteps coming upstairs from the hall. The steps were slow and hesitating, apparently those of an old man, and they were accompanied by the sound of laboured breathing, punctuated by various degrees of coughing.

'"Who's that coming upstairs?"

'There was no reply – we looked over the balusters, but although the coughing and wheezing came nearer and nearer, we saw no one. By this time we were too scared to move, our candlesticks fell to the ground, and we clung to each other in fear of the unknown. The steps paused for a moment beside us, as if the unseen owner of the feet had stopped to take breath. He then continued his upwards progress, until the coughing gradually died away and we heard no more.

'I implored my hostess not to go up to her bedroom, but to share mine, or any other on the first floor, but she refused, saying: "I have some Holy Water in my room, and with spiritual protection I fear nothing."

'So ended my ghost story, but some weeks later after my return to England, I received a letter from Lady Strickland:

'"After you left Plas yn Rhiw," she wrote, "I made cautious inquiries in the neighbourhood, and imagine what I've discovered! It appears that, at the end of the last century, the manor house was occupied by an old reprobate squire, who drank himself to death, and whose death-bed 'horrors' seem to have been something unthinkable. It is said that his earth-bound spirit occasionally revisits his home, vainly trying to obtain some gratification for his ceaseless thirst, so we were evidently favoured with one of his periodical returns."

'This explanation interested me greatly, but, let me admit, I am thankful I never saw, but only heard, what would doubtless have been a very dreadful psychic phenomena had it been permitted to materialize.'

As far as is known this is the last time this eerie manifestation has been heard. But then, of course, the house is no longer lived in. Perhaps the drunken squire's sick spirit still drags itself painfully through its former home unheard.

PARANORMAL PENRHYN

Penrhyn Castle is a magnificent folly, a 19th-century mansion built for an important local family in the medieval style. The architecture is mock Norman, the interior a glorious concoction of grand archways, stained glass and rich carving. Its reputation for paranormal activity is comparatively recent but now so frequently reported that there is an entire blog devoted to it (http://penrhynghosts.blogspot.co.uk). The blog is run by Caroline, who has worked at the house for many years and has therefore been able to glean a great deal of personal testimony from staff.

An illustration of Queen Victoria's visit to Penrhyn Castle in 1859

The blog makes fascinating reading. Numerous members of staff have reported feeling 'not alone' in empty rooms, glimpsing shadowy figures out of the corners of their eyes, or hearing ghostly footsteps. The footsteps sound as if they are made by someone with a limp. Several distinct apparitions have also been seen. A man and a girl were seen by a chef entering the tea-room kitchen but were nowhere to be found when he followed them in. Visitors have reported seeing the ghost of a 'housekeeper' near the tea room, a large bunch of keys hanging from her waist. The apparition of a maid, called 'Polly', who died in a fall down a flight of stairs, has been encountered from time to time, too.

An early 20th Century post card of
Penrhyn Castle

The railway museum in the courtyard seems particularly haunted. The ghost of a small boy has been seen running past the 'Charles Engine' before vanishing into a wall. On one occasion a former manager of the museum was approached by an angry visitor who complained that a 'mannequin' sitting in the 'Dinorwic Carriage' was 'too realistic' and it had frightened his son. Needless to say, on investigation the carriage was found to be empty. Others too have glimpsed a strange figure in this carriage.

The above three properties are all managed by the National Trust. Information on them can be found by visiting www.nationaltrust.org.uk and using the search tool for each property.

ODDNESS AT BODELWYDDAN

The grand building you see from the A55 Expressway near Rhyl is not the medieval castle you might imagine, but, like Penrhyn Castle, another fine example of Victorian Gothic revivalism. It was built around the heart of a 17th-century mansion. There is much to attract the visitor to Bodelwyddan Castle (www.bodelwyddan-castle.co.uk). Here can be found an offshoot gallery of the National Portrait Gallery, a Victorian 'games room', training trenches used in the First World War, a formal garden and woodland walks. The Castle is now a hotel, with a restaurant and coffee shops on site, too.

A walled-up skeleton may be a clue to the origin of some of the ghostly goings-on at Bodelwyddan Castle. © Richard Holland

Bodelwyddan Castle is one of those locations whose haunted reputation seems to have been recognised only since the advent of the TV programme *Most Haunted* and the many paranormal investigations which followed in its wake. The Castle now organises ghost-hunts for visitors. Nevertheless, the ghosts are claimed to have been in evidence long before then, possibly emerging first in 1829 after a restoration programme uncovered human bones behind a wall.

Ghosts now reported from Bodelwyddan Castle include a lady in one gallery, a soldier in another, and a blue lady in the Terrace Tea Room. In addition to more frequent reports of shadowy figures and a variety of unexplained noises and lights, visitors have also complained of having their hair pulled by invisible hands.

GRUESOME GWYDIR, QUESTIONABLE PLAS MAWR

Gwydir Castle, near Llanrwst, and Plas Mawr, in Conwy, are rare survivors of Welsh Tudor mansions which have remained largely unchanged down the centuries. Plas Mawr, indeed, is described as 'the finest surviving Elizabethan townhouse anywhere in Britain'.

Plas Mawr has a famous ghost story, but one which, sadly, is probably pure fiction. It tells of a 'Dr Dic' who was called to tend the lady of the house, who had gone into labour. Tragically, both the woman and her child died. The housekeeper was so frightened of the reaction of the master of the house when he returned that she locked Dr Dic into the bedroom to make sure

The fireplace up which 'Dr Dic' is supposed to have fled, according to the legend of Plas Mawr. © Richard Holland

he would be the one to break the terrible news. Equally alarmed, Dr Dic decided to make his escape and foolishly clambered up the chimney leading up from the fireplace. Or at least that is what he is supposed to have done – for he was never seen again.

Dr Dic's ghost is now said to haunt the house, and that chamber in particular. When I was researching my book *Haunted Wales: A Guide to Welsh Ghostlore* (History Press, 2011), however, I discovered an odd fact. The ghost story is said to be first recorded in a speech given by the then curator of the house, John Furness, to a visiting party of medical men. However, in 1907 the Cheshire historian Fletcher Moss visited Plas Mawr and was taken on a tour by Mr Furness, who was a friend of his.

Plas Mawr is one of the best-preserved Tudor townhouses in the country. A well-known ghost story of dubious provenance is attached to it. © Richard Holland

Admiring a secret passage in one of the wide fireplaces, Fletcher Moss said it was a shame there were no legends attached to it. Mr Furness had the perfect opportunity then to mention the ghost story, but did not do so. Did he come up with the legend of Dr Dic himself, having been given an unintentional hint to do so by Mr Moss?

The so-called 'Haunted Room' at Gwydir Castle, photographed in the early 20th century during a visit by historian Fletcher Moss.

Gwydir is an austere, haunted-looking mansion dripping with atmosphere. The former seat of one of the most important old families in North Wales, the Wynns, its ghostly legend may have a stronger claim to authenticity than that of Plas Mawr. Sir John Wynn is implicated in this yarn. He is said to have forced his attentions on a servant girl and then murdered her to keep her from talking. He hid her body in the chimney breast of a chamber still called the 'Ghost Room'. The apparition of the murdered girl has been seen in the room and in the passage outside it. Her killer has also been seen, on a staircase. The most persistent echo of this tragedy is the ghostly smell – the revolting stench of the decaying body which gave the murder away.

Almost as unpleasant is the sound of children crying, which has been reported as emanating from no certain source within the castle. A more friendly presence is reputed to be the dog which has taken to haunting the castle since its bones were found in the cellar in 1995. The origin of the procession of phantoms witnessed on the Great Terrace from time to time is a complete mystery, however.

Gwydir Castle is privately owned but open to the public (www.gwydircastle.co.uk). Be warned though: on the day I visited I was told off, not too politely, for taking photographs of its interior even though I wasn't using flash; there were no signs banning photography and my camera was in my hand when I bought the tickets; yet no warning was given. Cadw and the National Trust allow non-flash photography in their properties and the talking down to I endured from, I guess, some junior member of the family soured the visit considerably.

THE LADIES OF LLANGOLLEN

The Ladies of Llangollen may be the first identifiably lesbian couple in British and Irish history. In their day Irish aristocrats Lady Eleanor Butler and Sarah Ponsonby were simply seen as a quirky example of what was known as a 'romantic friendship' and it's impossible to be certain that their relationship was a

A rarely reproduced portrait of the Ladies of Llangollen towards the end of their lives together in Plas Newydd. It is these two indomitable spirits Dr Mary Gordon claimed to have met and conversed with long after their deaths.

sexual one. However, since they ran away together, endured a self-imposed exile from their families and lived together for the remainder of their lives, it seems not unlikely.

In 1778 they set up home in a purpose-built mansion, the site chosen for its views in what was then wildest Wales. Far from being shunned by society, the Ladies of Llangollen became national celebrities and were visited by the likes of the poets William Wordsworth, Percy Shelley and Lord Byron, ceramics giant Josiah Wedgwood and even the 'Iron Duke' of Wellington. They called their home Plas Newydd (literally 'the new mansion') and it remains a wonderful example of early Gothic revival architecture, boasting a wealth of original 16th-century carved oak. It is now run by Denbighshire County Council and is open to the public (www.denbighshire.gov.uk/en-gb/DNAP-73FFMH).

Plas Newydd was built specially for the Ladies of Llangollen and their spirits may linger here still. © *Richard Holland*

In the 1930s a psychologist by the name of Dr Mary Gordon claimed to have met and communicated with the spirits of the two Ladies after encountering them on a footpath above Plas Newydd. The spirits invited her to their home, but this meant that the elderly Dr Gordon, who was in her seventies, had to break into Plas Newydd by clambering in through a window (the house was at that time locked up and falling into disrepair). Dr Gordon claimed to have spent the entire night with the spirits of Lady Eleanor and Sarah Ponsonby, chatting until dawn. This ghostly conversation was written up in a book she published called *The Flight of the Wild Goose*.

It might still be possible to see the Ladies of Llangollen. According to one writer, Jack Hallam, they make a return visit to their beloved home every Christmas Eve and take a walk around the garden. However, for some inexplicable and ironic reason their ghosts can only be seen by men!

TWO HAUNTED CASTLES

A ruined castle is always atmospheric. Most have stood for hundreds of years and possess a rich history, including, of course a great deal of bloodshed. No wonder so many have gained a haunted reputation.

Ewloe Castle (Castell Ewlo) in Flintshire is arguably the most haunted in North Wales. Hidden deep in a wood, it's a mysterious and spooky-looking place even in broad daylight. This, like Powis Castle, described above, is a Welsh castle, not one built by invaders. However, by the late medieval period it was already in ruins. A great deal of paranormal activity has

Many strange things have been both seen and heard at Ewloe, a medieval castle spookily hidden away in a wood.
© Richard Holland

been reported from the castle, including strange glowing lights
and the steady tramp of marching feet. I spoke to a witness to
this latter phenomenon, Chris Preece, who heard it in company
with his uncle. It was daytime and the marching sound went on
for a considerable amount of time. They thought some sort of
pageant had been organised but no one arrived. It is believed
these may be the ghosts of a medieval English army which
marched on Ewloe with fateful and fatal results.

A Gothic ghostly legend is set at Rhuddlan Castle, now a magnificent ruin.
© Richard Holland

A former custodian claimed to hear ghostly singing emanating
from the ruins during thunderstorms. On one occasion he saw
what he believed to have been the origin of the singing: a
luminous white figure standing on top of one of the towers.

*The River Clwyd below Rhuddlan Castle, where a princess
tricked by a demonic spirit met her doom*

Rhuddlan Castle is one of North Wales's most impressive ruins, one of a chain of fortresses built on the orders of Edward I to help him keep an iron grip on Wales. Inside it is merely a shell (great for picnics!) but the walls and towers perched above the River Clwyd make Rhuddlan a picture-perfect castle. According to an old legend, the castle was the setting of an arranged marriage between a princess of North Wales and a prince of South Wales, a wedding intended to unite Wales. Everything went wrong, however, when a mysterious stranger called 'The Warrior Knight of the Blood Red Plume' rescued the Princess Erilda when she became lost in a fog-bound forest. He inveigled himself into the trust of the royal court and the affections of the princess – with fatal results.

The Warrior Knight convinced Erilda to elope with him. She did so, and ran away with him on the eve of her wedding, down to a boat moored on the Clwyd. The castle was roused and the couple were pursued. The Warrior Knight pressed a dagger into the frightened girl's hands. When she felt a hand grab her shoulder, she spun round, flailed out with the knife – and stabbed her father. She let out a scream of horror, which was drowned out by the mocking laughter of the Warrior Knight of the Blood Red Plume. The Knight announced that he was a demon, sent to frustrate the union between South and North Wales. With that, he transformed himself into a huge, scaly monster, and he dragged the hapless Erilda under the waters of the River Clwyd and down to hell.

Ever since that terrible night, states the legend, the spirit of Princess Erilda has been doomed to haunt Rhuddlan Castle, everlastingly pursued through the ruins by the demonic Warrior Knight of the Blood Red Plume.

TWO HAUNTED LIGHTHOUSES

When London-based ghost-hunter Richard Jones wrote his *Haunted Britain* book for the Automobile Association in 2010, he introduced me to a haunted location in North Wales which had previously escaped me: the South Stack Lighthouse, which is dramatically situated off the rocky west coast of Anglesey.

The ghost of a former keeper who tragically died in one of the worst storms in British history is still said to make his presence known at South Stack lighthouse.
© *Richard Holland*

According to Mr Jones, the ghost is of a Victorian keeper of the lighthouse, one Jack Jones (I presume no relation!). On October 25, 1853, a killer storm descended on Britain. It is remembered as the '*Royal Charter* Storm' after one of the more than two hundred ships it destroyed. The *Royal Charter* had sailed all the way from Australia and was almost in sight of its destination of Liverpool when the full blow of the tempest struck it off the east coast of Anglesey. The ship crashed against the rocks and four-hundred-and-fifty people drowned. The total number of fatalities across the UK numbered more than eight hundred.

On that fateful night Principal Keeper Henry Bowen was on duty, but recognising the seriousness of the situation, Jack Jones decided to go over to the lighthouse to give him a hand. The South Stack is an islet which in those days was connected to the main island by an iron bridge. Across this, buffeted by the gales and lashed by rain and raging surf, the brave keeper began to make his way. But he did not get far before a rock, torn from the cliff by the raging winds, smashed into his skull. Bowen was not expecting Jones and was astonished and horrified to find him the following morning, lying just outside the door to the lighthouse, covered in blood. He had managed to drag himself that far, but if he had shouted for help Bowen would not have heard him, for the fury of the storm would have drowned out his cries. Jack Jones died of his injuries three weeks later.

Today, occasional odd incidents experienced at South Stack lighthouse are blamed on the restless spirit of Jack Jones. They include disembodied footsteps, tapping on the window glass and the rattling of the front door by invisible hands.

There is a sense of mystery about lighthouses, something unearthly even, about the way they straddle two elements, the land and the sea. Deserted lighthouses are both evocative and eerie, so it's no wonder stories grow up around them. This is

*The Point of Ayr lighthouse hasn't been used since the 19th century but a
mysterious figure was seen inside it on a number of occasions.*
© Richard Holland

35

certainly the case with the now abandoned Point of Ayr lighthouse on the Flintshire coast. It stands on a stretch of sandy beach which, at low tide, is popular with walkers. In about the year 2000 reports began to be made of a ghostly figure seen in the locked-up building. Generally he was described as looking how a keeper might be expected to look: in a greatcoat and peaked cap. He would be seen standing behind the glass in broad daylight.

After a few reports were made to the BBC North-East Wales website, a lady wrote in to say that the 'ghost' was in fact her husband, who was paid to visit the empty 18th-century structure every day to check on its state of repair. This letter now seems to be missing from the website. Anyway, it didn't stop the rumours of ghosts, with the result that artist Angela Smith was commissioned to create a permanent 'ghost keeper', who now stands on the rail looking out over the beach.

HAUNTED CHURCHES

Churches are not infrequently haunted. We should not be surprised by this: not only are they often very old, but churches are, of course, centres of a community's spirituality, repositories of thousands of peoples' hopes and fears.

St Mary's
One of my own few spooky experiences took place at St Mary's Church in Mold (Yr Wyddgrug). I was in my teens at the time. 'Top Church', as it is known, was completed in 1501 and is a fine example of Perpendicular architecture. I visited one afternoon because it had been a long time since I'd been inside it and I wanted to examine some of the interior sculptures.

I passed through the porch but shyly waited outside the next door into the church because I could hear singing coming from within. A choir, I assumed, was practising. It certainly wasn't time for a service. After a few minutes there was a pause in the singing and I gingerly lifted the latch, wincing when it 'clunked' noticeably. I crept inside and was astonished to find that the church was entirely empty.

St Pedrog's

Spooky music also features in a story about Llanbedrog Church, Anglesey. Island resident Bunty Austin includes it in her book *Haunted Anglesey* (2005). She learnt of it from Mr John Roberts, one of her main informants of ghostly tales and folklore from Môn (to give Anglesey its proper Welsh name).

Mr Roberts told Bunty about a group of boys who went to catch rabbits one night in a big field above St Pedrog's Church. The dogs they took with them began to act in a peculiar way, cowering down and shivering rather than chasing pell-mell after the rabbits as they would normally do. Then the boys noticed that the church was brightly lit from inside. The faint sound of organ music could be heard emanating from it. They thought it unusual someone would be in the church practising the organ so late at night but were more concerned that someone might come out and chase them away.

A couple of weeks later they went back to the field with their lamps and dogs, and again they found the church illuminated and could hear the organ playing. Intrigued, they decided to find out who was in there. The windows were too high for them to peek inside, so they had no choice but to enter the church. As they cautiously began to lift the latch on the door the sound of the organ was 'booming'. As soon as the door creaked open, though, it stopped. The boys pushed their way in – only to find that the church was empty. No one was sitting at the organ. Nor could anyone have suddenly quit it and hidden themselves: the church was brightly lit and the organ in plain sight. Not only that, but the music had ended abruptly, 'as if someone had switched off a recording'. If someone had just stopped playing there would have been a gradual decaying of notes.

Completely spooked, the boys hurriedly left the church. One of them had the presence of mind to switch off the lights on his way out. They rejoined their dogs – which had refused to enter the churchyard – and then turned in amazement. The lights were back on in the church and the eerie sound of organ music was again to be heard.

Valle Crucis

The two examples above are not the only ones of ghostly music heard at sacred edifices. Unearthly singing has been reported off and on for centuries from the ruins of Valle Crucis Abbey near Llangollen. The earliest account dates from the 19th century, when two preachers took a rest among the ruins one misty early morning just before sun-up. They were entranced by a fine male voice singing firstly the *Dies Irae* and then the *De Profundis*. The moonlight was still bright and one of the ministers caught a glimpse of a man's shadow against one of the stone walls. Not wishing to disturb the singer, they settled themselves behind a chunk of masonry out of sight to listen to him.

The performance came to an end, after what should have been a matter of minutes, and the preachers were shocked to discover that the sun had come up and it was now broad daylight. They

Beautiful but eerie singing has been heard emanating from the romantic ruin of Valle Crucis Abbey. © Richard Holland

got to their feet and went in search of the singer to congratulate him, but he was nowhere to be found. Not knowing the exact time, the preachers were now rather agitated because they had been due to meet a horse and cart in Llangollen and they realised they would now be in danger of missing it. In fact, to their annoyance, they did miss it – they were three hours late! They subsequently learnt, however, that the cart had suffered an accident: it had overturned and a man was killed. Had the unearthly singing been sent to purposefully delay them, to save them from a dangerous crisis?

In 2003 I spoke to a woman who, unaware of this tradition, had also heard singing emanating from the abbey when, in 1950, she was staying at the neighbouring campsite. Coming back from Llangollen at about 10.30, she heard among the ruins 'beautiful music, singing like a choir, and an organ'. Her companion heard nothing. She told me: 'I can never get the memory of that beautiful music and that beautiful singing out of my head.'

However, no one believed her at the time, so she was delighted when some years later she spotted a letter in the *Liverpool Echo* (her local paper at the time) which went some way towards confirming her tale. The letter was from a cyclist who also heard singing coming from Valle Crucis while he was repairing his bike. In a direct echo of my informant's experience, his friend was unable to hear the voice.

When I was researching my book *Haunted Clwyd* (1992), I received a letter from a Wrexham resident who also witnessed something strange at Valle Crucis. Walking past the ruined abbey with her aunt she was 'amazed to see in front of the Abbey the ground light up in a large circle of the most dazzling

*The spirit of Owain Glyndŵr appeared at the now-ruined
Valle Crucis Abbey and spoke to a former abbot here*

light – apparently emanating from the ground'. She continued: 'In the middle of the circle there was some kind of golden object, several feet high, and walking about quite a number of human figures, garbed in wonderful golden costumes with golden kind of helmets on their heads.'

Her aunt was unable to see anything unusual – this lack of sensitivity on the part of the witnesses' companions seems a common theme – and after a minute or so the vision vanished. No sound accompanied this rather splendid scene and it's tempting to wonder whether the lovely music heard by other witnesses originally accompanied it.

Before we leave Valle Crucis Abbey I must mention the tradition that Owain Glyndŵr's spirit appeared here to a former abbot. After his defeat by the forces of Henry IV in 1410, Glyndŵr disappeared from history. The implication of this story is that he died soon afterwards. His spirit delivered a prophecy to the abbot: that the English throne would be taken in time by rulers of Welsh descent. This took place after the Battle of Bosworth when Richard III was defeated by Henry Tudor. Tudor was descended from the Tewdwrs of Penmynydd. When Henry was crowned Henry VII in 1485 the Tudor dynasty began.

Strata Florida

Strata Florida Abbey (Abaty Ystrad Fflur), near Pontrhydfendigaid, Ceredigion, was, like Valle Crucis, a house of Cistercian monks but its ruins are far less extensive than those of its Denbighshire sister. The name translates as 'Valley of the Flowers', although 'Fflur' is actually the name of the river that runs past the abbey. This was doubtless a very pleasant spot when the Strata Florida was founded way back in the 12th century.

In common with many other ecclesiastical houses, the ghost is that of a monk. He is said to appear at the eastern end of the abbey ruins on Christmas Eve. He is possibly still carrying out the Christmastide service at the altar (which is now missing), just as he did for many years when alive. The gleam of lighted candles has also been seen within the ruins after dark.

Strata Florida is linked with another legend, that of the Holy Grail. The nearby mansion of Nanteos once held a little wooden bowl of great age which they claimed was the cup Christ used at the Last Supper. According to tradition, the bowl or cup had been brought from the Holy Land to Strata Florida, and then came into the possession of the local lords of the manor on the Dissolution of the Monasteries. An important medieval Welsh poet, Dafydd ap Gwilym, is believed to be buried under a venerable yew tree in the grounds. Today a plaque set up in the midst of its spreading branches commemorates the poet.

St Mor's and St Deiniol's

Fancy buying a (formerly) haunted church? This charming Gothic edifice in the village of Llanfor, near Bala in Gwynedd, is no longer used as a place of worship and has been put up for sale by The Church in Wales. Hundreds of years ago there was another period when sacred service was abandoned at the church but this wasn't due to lack of interest: the local people were desperate to worship there. Trouble is, it had been invaded by a ghost, who set up residence in it. During the spook's unwanted incumbency, preaching took place in the village pub!

The churchyard at Llanfor. Once upon a time a ghostly presence took up residence in Llanfor church and had to be forcibly evicted. © Richard Holland

As ghosts go, the one at Llanfor was fairly civilised. He was dressed as a gentleman, in fine clothes and a three-cornered hat, and would take pleasant evening strolls around the countryside, when not making loud noises in the church and illuminating it with a weird glow. But as Victorian folklorist Elias Owen puts it: 'Although harmless, he was a great terror to the neighbourhood.'

'Two gentlemen skilled in divination' were brought in to exorcise the ghost. There are two versions of how this was accomplished. In each a battle of wills takes place between the exorcists and the reluctant spirit until they succeed in conjuring him into animal form before 'laying' him beneath the waters of a pool in the River Dee, just as evil spirits were 'laid' in the Red Sea in Biblical times.

In one version, the ghost is made to take the shape of a cockerel. It is carried to the pool by a horse, which clears the distance from the church in two mighty bounds. In the other version, he takes the form of a pig. This shocked one elderly parishioner, who cried out: 'Duw anwyl! Mochyn yn yr eglwys (Dear God! A pig in the church).' By breaking the silent solemnity of the ceremony, she made the phantom pig 'exceedingly fierce' and he threw both the exorcist and the horse he was riding right over the church. Despite this tantrum, he was eventually banished to his watery prison.

St Etheldreda's

The church at Hyssington is the only one in Wales dedicated to St Etheldreda, an Anglo-Saxon princess. This little church is tucked away in a secluded village right on the Powys–Shropshire border. It too saw a battle of wills between ghost-layers and ghost, although this one was a much more alarming entity.

Many years ago, according to legend, the countryside round about was the haunt of a hideous supernatural creature. It took the shape of a giant bull without any skin, and its bellows after dark used to have the local populace hiding under their bedcovers. Seven brave clergymen got together to deal with the 'Roaring Bull', as it was known. They gathered at St Etheldreda's to 'pray the devil down'. The furious Roaring Bull, agonised by the prayers of the holy men, charged up to the church and barged its way in. In an attempt to intimidate the parsons, the horrible thing made itself bigger and bigger and bigger. It got so big that the walls of the church cracked. The clergymen persevered, however, and 'prayed down' the monster until it was tiny. They then trapped it in a snuff box and buried it under a nearby bridge.

*Once upon a time evidence of an attack by a monstrous ghostly creature could
be seen in Hyssington church but unfortunately it was removed during a
19th-century restoration project.*
© *Richard Holland*

The Roaring Bull never troubled the land again. Until a rather severe restoration in Victorian times removed them, cracks in the walls were pointed out in the church as proof of the story.

St Nicholas's

The legend relating to the parish church of Montgomery in Powys is one of the most celebrated from Wales, largely because it is so well authenticated. The 'ghost' is no longer to be seen, but it was visible for several decades and was witnessed by hundreds if not thousands of people. The spot where it appeared can still easily be found today because there are not one but two signs showing where it was.

In 1821 a man named John Newton was hanged for highway robbery. Throughout his trial he insisted upon his innocence and many people believed that he was indeed guiltless of the accusation. In their minds subsequent events proved they had been right to doubt the evidence. Newton was an Englishman, and therefore an outsider, who was employed as estate manager for a widow at nearby Chirbury. Before Newton took over, the estate was in sad decline and a neighbouring landowner called Pearce had been looking forward to acquiring it. Newton improved things considerably, thereby frustrating Pearce's ambitions. Not only that, but an understanding was clearly growing between Newton and the widow's daughter Jane. If he married Jane, he might well inherit the estate. Others had had their eye on Jane and her inheritance, in particular a young farmer called Parker, who had convinced himself he was to be the lucky man. But Jane much preferred Newton.

It was Pearce and Parker who brought the charge of robbery with violence against John Newton. They said he had tried to

Two little signs still show the position of the so-called 'Robber's Grave'
in Montgomery churchyard. © Richard Holland

hold them up on the road but they had succeeded in overpowering him. Their version of events was believed and Newton was executed – in the midst of a thunderstorm that sounded like the rage of heaven to those who were present. On hearing the guilty verdict brought against him, Newton made a bold statement. He asserted that proof of his innocence would be found on his grave, for the turf would not lie easy over such a wronged man. He said that for an entire generation no grass would grow on his grave.

For at least three decades this was certainly the case. John Newton's last resting place in the churchyard of St Nicholas's, Montgomery, was 'clearly marked as a sterile patch about the size and shape of a coffin'. In 1852 a Rev Mostyn Price wrote: 'Thirty years have passed away and the grass has not covered his grave.'

For Newton's words to come true was, as you can imagine, a sensation in the neighbourhood. His accusers, Pearce and Price, were afterwards looked upon askance by everyone. Borne down no doubt with guilt, one became a drunkard and the other 'wasted away from the earth'. Several people tried to 'break the curse' by laying down fresh turf over the grave or sprinkling it liberally with grass seed. Nothing worked. The grave remained stubbornly barren. Even a century-and-a-half later 'The Robber's Grave', as it became known, was readily apparent, although the extent of the bare earth had by this time shrunk down to a smaller, cruciform shape. Today grass does now grow on The Robber's Grave and also a rose bush, planted perhaps as a symbol of John Newton's innocence more than a hundred years after he was sent to the gallows.

HAUNTED HOSTELRIES

Pubs and hotels are not infrequently haunted. Many are very old and have seen a lot of life – and death, too. Pubs in particular are often at the heart of their communities, along with the church, and this might be why they seem to attract so much paranormal activity. Over the years I have investigated several haunted pubs in North Wales.

Talacre Arms

The Talacre Arms in Holywell, Flintshire, is a modern pub in a historic area, nearly opposite the important medieval pilgrim site of St Winifred's Well. When I visited the pub some years ago, I was told the ghost liked to play pranks, including one familiar to landlords in ghost-infested taverns: it would turn the pumps off and on and move barrels around in the cellar.

One morning, the licensees found three large bottles of spirits missing from the locked bar. The bottles had been attached to optics upside-down, but there was no spillage on the floor and the optics each still contained a full measure, showing that the bottles hadn't been upended to remove them. This was a difficult, if not impossible feat, and there were lots of other bottles standing around that would have been a lot easier to pinch.

As well as the landlord, I spoke to a few regulars, who told me that the spook's party piece was making light bulbs drop on to the pool table in the middle of games. These were not bayonet bulbs which had sprung loose: they had been tightly screwed in. In my *Haunted Clwyd* (1992), I noted: 'One evening a bulb in a newly fitted screw-in socket fell on to the pool table, extremely hot. It was removed and another fitted. Five minutes later this too fell from the screw-in socket. A third was fitted – and promptly exploded. A local, John James, said he found this particularly unnerving because it only seemed to happen when it was his turn to take a shot!'

Boar's Head

My local when I was a young man was also haunted, or rather became so. All had been quiet until restructuring work was carried out on the building, in which the position of the entrance door was changed and the bar areas made open plan. For some unknown reason, building work often brings out the spooks.

The Boar's Head is an old pub in Mold town centre. At the time I'm speaking of the landlords were the Armishaws, a family I got to know very well. I was told of a number of spooky activities in the building, including an eerie low whistling, a mirror which suddenly flew off a wall, and an indistinct figure which would be seen drifting from the recently bricked-up front door towards the rear of the pub, where the landlord's accommodation had formerly been situated. On one notable occasion, members of the family, who lived above the pub, distinctly heard horses stamping and moving about in the courtyard, even though horses had not been stabled there for the best part of a century.

One does have to be careful with ghost stories told about pubs, though, because publicans often see potential in the publicity a resident ghost might generate. After the Armishaws moved on, a succession of landlords and landladies took over at the Boar's Head. One of them enhanced its haunted reputation with accounts of numerous apparitions and poltergeist activity and she took photos of blurry 'ghosts' in the cellar. A subsequent

A ghost suddenly manifested in the Boar's Head pub in Mold after building work was carried out. © Richard Holland

landlady, learning of all this from customers, not unreasonably saw the value in holding a 'Psychic Night' in the pub with an (alleged) medium. Staying in a quieter part of the bar, I received running reports from the landlady on all the 'grounded spirits' the medium was supposedly discovering. One of these was a 'Roman soldier'. I pointed out that Mold was one of the few places the Romans didn't visit. This was then rapidly amended to a 'roaming soldier'. I couldn't help but admire the man's quick thinking!

Sadly, at the time of writing it looks as if the Boar's Head may now be closed permanently and turned into flats. If so, I wonder whether the building work will lead to further ghostly activity?

Golden Lion

Situated in Rossett, one of the show villages of Wrexham County Borough, this charming old pub has a reputation for ghosts dating back several hundred years. In the 17th century an attempted murderer was hanged and his body then hung in chains from a gibbet on Rossett green. This grisly monument got on the nerves of the villagers, so one night a party of men chopped it down and buried the crow-pecked skeleton on the green. Ever since then the criminal's ghost, known as 'Old Jeffrey', was believed to patrol the village after dark.

I uncovered a snippet in a long-defunct journal that wood from this gibbet was incorporated into an outbuilding at the Golden Lion, so I went to take a look. The (slightly puzzled) staff very kindly allowed me to investigate and sure enough we found a beam in a store house out the back with a large, rusty staple sticking out of it. The presence of this reworked gibbet may have encouraged talk of a ghost centuries ago but staff were able to confirm spooky goings-on in the pub, mainly of the 'odd noises', 'things being moved' variety. An apparition of a man has been reported from time to time standing at the top of a flight of stairs. He seems a friendly presence, however, so perhaps he isn't 'Old Jeffrey'.

On the day I visited I learnt of a haunted bedroom which they no longer used for guests due to complaints of disturbed nights. On the day I visited, a brewery area manager happened to be on site and he told me about the night he stayed in the room. He didn't believe in ghosts and certainly didn't expect the tussle he had with something that insisted upon trying to pull the bedclothes off the bed.

He was unaware, until I told him, that this behaviour is a common feature of poltergeist cases. He told me that despite the struggle he found it impossible to open his eyes to see what was in the room with him. He didn't think it was fear that was forcing them closed but some outside agency. His experience sounds a bit like 'night terror', when people unable to wake up suffer hallucinations. This little-understood phenomenon may explain a number of ghost experiences.

Black Lion

Another strange occurrence took place at this rather isolated little pub near the village of Babell in Flintshire. I recently met a former policeman who told me of the night in the 1970s when his station received a call from the Black Lion's landlord. It was nearly midnight and the landlord and his wife were distressed by the fact that someone was knocking frantically on the front door and calling for help. The stranger had an American accent. 'Well, why don't you let him in and find out what's wrong?' asked the policeman.

'Because we're looking down at the door right now and there's nobody there,' replied the terrified publican. 'Listen' – and he must have held the receiver out of the window because, sure enough, on the other end of the line my informant could hear the faint sounds of knocking and a male voice yelling to be let in.

He and a colleague drove round there, too late to catch the invisible man – he'd ceased his hammering – but in time to be unnerved by what he described as a 'very weird atmosphere' about the place. He told me the landlord and his wife were obviously upset and he had no doubt in his mind that something genuinely weird had just taken place. The only suggestion offered to explain the haunting – if such it was – is that a small airbase had been situated nearby during the war and had been used by Canadian airmen: was this the origin of the 'American' voice, its cries for help recalling some forgotten tragedy of the 1940s?

Llyndir Inn

The Llyndir was built in the 13th century and sports a thatched roof, a rare feature in North Wales. It found itself on national

Daily Post 21st April 1960

HIS THROAT, AND CLAIMS:

I brushed with ghost at inn on Denbigh moors

A THIRTY-SIX-YEAR-OLD St. Helens man, Mr Raymond Kenyon, of Gladstone Street, who has just returned from his Easter holiday in North Wales, claims that he has had a brush with a ghost in the tiny 731-year-old thatched village inn at remote Henllan, Denbighshire.

Mr Kenyon said he felt cold fingers on his throat, his bed was rocked from side to side, the bedclothes dragged off and he heard the sound of a struggle in the room where he slept under the eaves. It was in this room, legend says, where a long-dead landlord of the inn strangled his wife.

In this room over the past few years, says the proprietess, blonde Mrs Silvie Michallow, scores of visitors have experienced hauntings of various natures, and the legend of the tavern on the edge of the Denbigh moors has spread throughout Wales.

Mr Kenyon said yesterday he dilled off to sleep on Saturday, and then: "I woke up feeling cold and my body was covered with goose pimples. Then I felt an invisible force confronting me from where the resting table stands about two feet from the bottom of the bed—and the floorboards were making loud creaking noises as if one or two persons were struggling.

Stay feminine, says Duchess

THE Duchess of Kent, opening Sheppey Technical School for Girls at Sheerness, Kent, yesterday, said: "However important a successful career may be, it matters far more that a woman should remain essentially feminine.

Mr Kenyon in the room where he claims he came up against the

The original press report of Mr Kenyon's brush with the ghost of the Llyndir Inn at Henllan

television in 1960 after a guest staying in the inn told the press about his creepy overnight stay there. Mr Raymond Kenyon told *The Daily Post*: 'I woke up feeling cold and my body was covered in goose pimples. Then I felt an invisible force confronting me from where the dressing table stands at the bottom of the bed and the floorboards were making loud creaking noises as if one or two persons were struggling. Then I felt a pressure like a cold hand on my throat.'

Mr Kenyon dared the room for a second night but again heard the sounds of struggling, felt 'icy-cold fingers' on his face, his bed shook and something dragged the bedclothes on to the floor (see also the Golden Lion, above). The landlord at the time responded: 'This kind of thing is quite usual. Almost every day I feel taps on my shoulders as I am cooking or cleaning the place.'

Three weeks prior to Mr Kenyon's report, a member of the inn's darts team had been pushed down the stairs by someone invisible, and not long before that a group of visitors were scared away by the 'tappings, groanings and icy fingers in the night'. The tale given to explain all this unpleasantness was that a woman had been strangled to death by her husband in the haunted room centuries before. Her ghost, that of a woman in a blue (others say white) gown, has also been seen.

Bull Hotel

The Bull has been providing comfortable beds and serving up splendid food and drink in Llangefni, Anglesey, since the early 19th century. This makes it a comparatively modern building compared to some of the hostelries described above, but it stands on the site of a much older inn. Bunty Austin, author of *Haunted Anglesey* (2005), learnt of the ghostly goings-on at the Bull first-hand when she and her late husband Walt stayed here as a young couple. At dead of night they both witnessed 'a globular orange light about the size and shape of a tennis ball' floating round their darkened room. Some years later the Austins came to live on Anglesey and Bunty found out more about the ghosts at the Bull.

She was told that on an upstairs landing the apparition of an old woman in a rocking chair has been seen, rocking peacefully and as solid and real-looking as a living person, other than the fact that she is dressed in clothing of a past century. The hotel appears to be haunted from top to bottom. Eerie laughter has been heard emanating from the corner of a cellar which is so deep it may date from the medieval building pre-dating the Bull. High in the attic rooms there is a particularly friendly ghost: a little brown-and-white terrier. When renovations were being carried out at the hotel in the 1990s, the dog would approach men working on the roof and then scamper silently off. The men assumed it was a real dog until they saw it running straight through a wall.

Ruthin Castle Hotel

The medieval Ruthin Castle is now an atmospheric ruin behind the luxury hotel, which has been created within a handsome former country house once belonging to the Churchill family. Winston Churchill's mother, Lady Randolph Churchill, lived here for many years. The original castle was presided over in the 15th century by a Norman baron named Reginald de Grey, whose arrogance and deceitful behaviour led to the uprising by

*The gloomy medieval ruins of Ruthin Castle are haunted
by a murderess. © Richard Holland*

national Welsh hero Owain Glyndŵr. Remnants of these good old days are a Whipping Pit at the base of one of the towers and a Drowning Pit where de Grey could enjoy the sight of his enemies struggling to keep their heads above water as the river was drained into it.

The ruins are said to be haunted by a ghost who also dates from these turbulent times. Known as the 'Grey Lady' because of the colour of her gown, she is a gentle, mournful spirit, quite unlike the fiery character she must have possessed in life. When she found her husband, a Norman knight, having an affair with another woman she wasted no time in getting rid of her rival – with an axe! She was executed for the murder and, denied burial in consecrated ground, was laid to rest in the battlements. The 'Grey Lady's Grave' can still be seen today.

I have also heard reports of a ghostly woman being seen in the hotel by staff working early shifts. Whether she is the Grey Lady, exploring beyond her usual domain, or some other apparition it is hard to say, for the ghost has merely been glimpsed. Ruthin Castle Hotel has long been celebrated for its popular 'medieval banquets'. The banqueting hall has become an established venue for organised ghost-hunts and overnight vigils, with the usual round of phenomena from such events being reported, such as strange noises, spooky voices and mysterious lights. A book published in the 1980s refers to one other ghost at Ruthin Castle, that of a knight in armour wearing only one gauntlet. He sounds like a character from a Gothic romance but I have been unable to track down the original source of this spook.

A ghost has also been seen in the Ruthin Castle Hotel, a former Victorian mansion attached to the medieval castle. Odd things have been reported from the banqueting hall, too. © *Richard Holland*

HOUNDS THAT HAUNT

In 1929 the folklorist T Gwynne Jones wrote: 'My grandmother declared that as she and my grandfather were riding on horseback from Ruthin one evening, in passing a roadside house, the nag suddenly shied and pressed to the hedge. At that moment a very tall mastiff was passing on the other side. My grandfather, who rode behind, saw nothing and his horse had not been startled. They had just come to live in the district and

Arthur Conan Doyle's celebrated novel The Hound of the Baskervilles *was inspired by tales of spectral Black Dogs haunting the British countryside. They have often been seen in Wales.*

only got to know afterwards that the house had the reputation of being haunted.'

Phantoms of huge hounds, usually black in colour and often sporting grimly glowing red eyes, are a species of spook reported throughout the British Isles. Generally they are simply known as 'Black Dogs' but in Wales they were sometimes given the rather obscure name 'Gwyllgi' (of which the best translation seems to be 'Dog of the Twilight') and also 'Cŵn Annwn' ('Hounds of the Underworld'). Another example was apparently encountered on a wild stretch of heath near the village of Cynwyd in Denbighshire. It followed home an old soldier, who described it as being of 'fearsome visage and bloodshot eye'. It kept 'just astern' of him all the way, and the poor man was in 'the horrible cold sweat of a nightmare', expecting it to pounce on him at any moment. However, these Black Dogs rarely cause harm and this one left the old soldier unmolested to his door.

Similar spectres have also turned up in Anglesey, according to correspondents to my 'Wales of the Unexpected' column in the *North Wales Daily Post* (later published in book form in 2005). One was seen by the late father of Mr William Owen, when he was cycling near Llanfechell. According to Mr Owen: 'It was a fierce-looking creature the size of a calf. It did not venture to attack in any way but it was just following my father like a shadow. However fast my father rode his bike, the dog managed to keep a few yards ahead. When they came to the junction of the Cemaes Bay to Holyhead road it simply vanished!'

Another was seen by the late husband of Mrs Jones-Williams, who kindly wrote to tell me of his experience when, as a small boy, he was walking down a footpath near Llanfachraeth with his father. They were startled to see 'a big black dog' blocking their way. They were even more startled when, gingerly approaching it, the animal 'vanished into thin air'.

An unusual variety of Black Dog haunted Pen Parcau, near Aberystwyth. According to a rather sad legend, a giant was riding his horse at tremendous speed over Pen Parcau, with one hand holding the reins, the other his dog's leash. But the unfortunate dog couldn't keep up with him and finally it collapsed. The giant still kept charging on ahead, dragging the poor pooch along behind him until its head was pulled off! The headless hound is said to still be seen running across the spot where it met its unhappy end.

A few years ago I was delighted to talk to somebody who had personally seen one of these spectres, or at least something very like one. The witness, Mr Malcolm Jones, does not believe in ghosts and is therefore not entirely convinced that what he saw one evening in 1971 was of supernatural origin. Nevertheless, he admitted to me that the encounter had left him shaken, and recalling it even after all these years 'made his hairs stand up'. His 'Gwyllgi', if such it was, walked across his path as he was making his way home one evening to Brymbo, near Wrexham. He said it was huge, much bigger than a dog but smaller than a cow, and that it had the shape of a lurcher dog: long, lean and with a pointed nose. It was getting dark and the creature was therefore entirely black.

Mr Jones recalled: 'It didn't make a sound, just stopped in the middle of the road and seemed to stare at me, although I couldn't see its eyes. Then it lost interest and carried on walking across the lane, where it disappeared into the vegetation on the

*The Red Path, in Brymbo, Wrexham, where a frightening,
bestial spook was seen in the 1980s. © Richard Holland*

other side. That's what made it so spooky. Apart from looking weird, it didn't behave like an ordinary animal. The way it looked at me, as if it was weighing me up. It wasn't fazed by a human presence and most animals are.'

The next day Mr Jones returned to the place where saw the thing but could find no opening for it to pass through on either side of the lane. What especially interested me about this sighting, in addition to its recent date, was the fact that it linked with the most bizarre and dramatic account of an apparition it has been my good fortune to discover.

On the same evening I met Mr Jones, I also met Mrs J and Mrs S (both names on record). Meeting these two ladies came about after years of trying to pin down a rumour I'd heard of sightings of something very weird indeed in a village near Wrexham in the 1980s. Thanks to a friend, Jonathan Edwards, I discovered the village must be Brymbo, from the vague description I'd received of it, and thanks to his mother Sylvia I was introduced to two of the witnesses to what I later couldn't resist calling 'The Beast of Brymbo'.

One bright, moonlit night in December, 1985, Mrs J and Mrs S were walking to their homes up the 'Red Path' in the centre of the village when they saw something glowering down at them from an outcrop of sandstone overlooking the footpath.

'It was cow-like, standing on its hind legs and at least six-foot tall,' Mrs J told me. 'It was a light brown colour and smooth-haired. There were two little bumps where you might expect horns. We could see it clearly because it was illuminated by the moon and the streetlights. It just stood there, frowning down at us with its eyes wrinkled up. Its hooves were sort of dangling down in front of it.

'We ran up the Red Path but then realised it could easily cut us off at the top. When we got there, though, it had vanished.'

I know of another sighting in which two small children had returned home one afternoon in great distress because they had been frightened by 'a cow standing on its hind legs'. This account, which I heard in 1987 shortly after it had occurred, came to me very much second-hand but the vague description I was given of a path connecting two parts of a village near Wrexham is certainly a good fit with the Red Path in Brymbo, and the nature (or rather supernature) of both sightings would be too much of a coincidence for it to be anything else.

I have no doubt about the veracity of the witnesses I met. The two women are convinced the 'Beast' couldn't possibly have been a costume, which, if it were a hoax, only leaves some sort of doll as an explanation. However, there isn't much in the way of cover on the Red Path to hide something so bulky as quickly as would be needed and it seems unlikely that a hoaxer would perpetrate the same stunt two years apart, once on a bitter winter's night and again in broad daylight. Then there is Mr Jones's sighting to consider. This took place more than twenty years earlier and yet his description would fit quite well with 'The Beast of Brymbo' walking on all fours.

All three witnesses' sightings had remained private and certainly unpublished until they kindly told me about them, and this makes their accounts of this very weird apparition all the more compelling.

THE GLOOMIEST GHOSTS OF ALL

Among the most frequently reported of all ghostly goings-on in Wales, certainly in past centuries, are a variety of phenomena collectively known as 'Tolaeth'. Tolaeth are supernatural warnings of death or some other coming calamity. The origin of the word Tolaeth is uncertain but may have some connection to 'teulu', the Welsh word for 'family', since these are often personal spooks, involving family members.

The Tolaeth were said to have been brought into being by the patron saint of Wales, St David (or Dafydd), who prayed to the Almighty that his people should have some warning of their imminent death so that they would have time to right any wrongs and prepare themselves for the afterlife. This may be why such phenomena were more common in Wales than elsewhere in the UK.

Corpse Candles

Corpse Candles, or Canwyllau Cyrff in the original Welsh, are among the commonest of the Tolaeth. The 19th-century Welsh folklorist Elias Owen described them as 'a light like that of a candle, which was said to issue from the house where a death was about to occur, and take the course of the funeral procession to the burial place. This was the usual way of proceeding, but this mysterious light was also said to wend its way to the abode of a person about to die.'

According to another folklorist, John Ceredig Davies, writing a couple of decades later: 'Sometimes the light was seen carried by a spectral representation of the dying person, and it was even

An old engraving of a Corpse Candle, or Canwyll Cyrff, one of the many death omens formerly believed in in Wales.

thought possible to recognise that person by standing near the water and watching as the apparition crossed over it. Another way of recognising the dying person was to stand at the church porch watching the candle entering the building.'

Corpse Candles have been reported for hundreds of years. John Lewis, Justice of the Peace in Aberystwyth, wrote in 1656 of 'the strange and unusual appearance of lights (called in Welch dead men's candles) before mortality.' He added: 'This is ordinary in most of our counties . . . seen before death and often observed to part from the very bodies of the persons, all along the way to the place of burial, and infallibly death will ensue.'

Mr Lewis had a personal experience – or very nearly – with Corpse Candles. He wrote: 'On a time, some years past, it was told me . . . that two Candles was [*sic*] seen, one little and a great one passing the Church way, under my house. My wife was then great with child, and near her time, and she feared of it, and it begot some fear in us about her; but just about a week after, herself first came to me (as something joyed that the fear might be over) and said (as true it was) an old man, and a child of the neighbourhood passed that same way to be buried.'

A ghostly light shines above the body of anyone unfortunate enough to have drowned in the River Dee. At Holt Bridge, seen in the picture, the terrified cries of two little boys deliberately drowned beneath it are said to still be heard

An intriguing sidelight (if you'll pardon the pun) refers to the River Dee, which flows through North-East Wales until it reaches the sea between Flintshire and the Wirral. Another belief stated in the 17th century was that: 'When any Christian is drowned in the River Dee, there will appear over the water where the corpse is, a light, by which means they do find the body. And it is therefore called the holy Dee.' (In fact the 'holy Dee' had also been sacred in pre-Christian times.)

Elias Owen was told of a man who met a Corpse Candle in a lane near his home. The weird glowing light alarmed him and he lashed out at it with his stick, bursting it into countless sparks, which then reassembled themselves. The frightened man hurried home, unaware that the Corpse Candle he'd encountered was a warning of his own imminent death. When, some time later, the man's funeral procession was wending its way down the lane where he had seen the candle, the bier carrying the coffin suddenly broke, tumbling the casket to the ground. This took place at the precise spot where he had shattered the Corpse Candle with his stick.

Finally, moving into more modern times, one of Britain's most famous ghost-hunters, Elliott O'Donnell, once recounted a tale to an equally celebrated colleague, Peter Underwood, about a very literal Corpse Candle which manifested at Aberystwyth. The candle itself was a perfectly ordinary one but dimmed and glowed with an eerie blue flame, unnerving a young woman, O'Donnell's informant, who was sleeping in the room where it stood. She blew the candle out, but it relighted itself minutes later! The girl tried again, but in vain – so she hid her head under the bedclothes, shutting out the cold blue light which insisted on filling her room.

The next morning, expecting to be laughed at, she described her experience to an old servant woman, who proved anything but mirthful on the subject. The Canwyll Cyrff was a death omen, she said, and someone in the family was doomed to die! On this occasion, Death pointed his scythe at the young woman's aunt, who passed away unexpectedly in her sleep a scant few days later.

Phantom funerals

These are unusual in that they are ghosts of the future. Phantom funerals would take the form of apparitions that exactly mirrored a funeral procession shortly due to take place. They were reported much more often in South Wales than in North Wales. According to D E Jenkins, writing about Beddgelert, Gwynedd, at the end of the 19th century: 'They only appeared before the death of some well-known or distinguished person in the district, or someone noted for his wickedness or ungodliness.'

Mr Jenkins continues: 'The funeral was not so often seen as heard, invariably coming from the house where death was to take place. The crowd was made up of the spirits of those who would be attending the funeral, each spirit taking up the exact position which its owner would take on the day of the burial. If horses and traps were to be in the procession, they would be distinctly heard.

'When one happened to meet one of these ghostly processions, the best thing was to silently wait by the roadside until the whole concourse had passed by, for fear they might trample him under foot, or take him on to the churchyard – an ordeal that generally ended in insanity.'

Last century a Phantom Funeral was followed by a man all the way to the porch of Corwen churchyard. The photograph shows the medieval preacher's cross near the front porch. © Richard Holland

Another important collector of folk tales and accounts of the supernatural in Wales, Marie Trevelyan, learnt of two encounters with phantom funerals in North Wales. One took place in Corwen, Denbighshire, and was told to Trevelyan by the witness first-hand. He said: 'I was coming home from a neighbouring village, when I suddenly heard wailing sounds a short distance in advance. I paused and listened, and suddenly found myself borne backward in a funeral procession. I distinctly saw the coffin and recognised one or two persons in the crowd beside me. With the procession I was borne on to the ancient parish church, and not far from the doorway saw a well-known Dissenting minister approaching and joining us. Then the whole phantom vanished.

'I was greatly frightened, and on reaching home promptly related my experiences. About fourteen days later a friend of ours died in Corwen. I went to the funeral, and, arriving rather late, was pressed backward in the crowd. Near the old church a well-known Dissenting minister joined the procession, and in it I recognised other people who appeared previously as phantoms.'

The other one occurred in Ruabon (Rhiwabon), in Wrexham. The uncle of Trevelyan's informant had been hurrying home at twilight on a cold day in December when a funeral procession loomed out of the gloom. He stood back to let it pass. As the cortege proceeded past him, he could clearly make out the coffin on its bier and the mourners, including a doctor and a tradesman he knew well. He could also hear the people singing, but although he recognised the tune, he was unable to make out the words. The puzzled man watched as the funeral made its way towards the church – and then past it. As the procession reached a house just beyond the church, it vanished. Realising he had seen something unearthly, the witness rushed home and told his family what he had seen.

The story continues: 'About six weeks later my uncle happened to be in Ruabon in the twilight, and a funeral procession passed the spot where he had seen the phantom mourners. Curiously, the real funeral passed the church, and halted at the house he had seen in his vision. In the procession the doctor and tradesman were seen as before. The body was that of a person who had died in the South of England, and was conveyed to the house of the deceased, there to remain until the next day. This explained the remarkable circumstance of a funeral in the late twilight.'

Unearthly sounds
Inexplicable knocks, taps and raps were also considered portents of a coming death, especially if they took place near somebody's sick bed. Many carpenters would tell of hearing the sounds of sawing and banging coming from their workshops in the middle of the night. This was a sure sign that their services would shortly be required – to construct a coffin. This eerie phenomenon has been reported within living memory on Anglesey.

There is also a tale of a tailor who lived many years ago in old Carnarvonshire, now part of Gwynedd, who said odd noises would warn him of the imminent death of a customer. One day, he said, he was repairing the breeches of a huntsman when he heard a mysterious rapping or tapping on his work-table. If he set the breeches aside for a few moments, while threading a needle or cutting a piece of cloth, for example, the sounds ceased, but when he took up his work again, the tapping was resumed. In this way he claimed to be able to foretell the deaths of his neighbours.

The Rev Elias Owen was told that it was not uncommon in North Wales for people who were close to death to say they have heard 'sweet voices singing in the air, and they have called the attention of the watchers to the angelic sounds and requested perfect silence so as not to lose a single note of the heavenly song'.

He continues: 'A young lad, whom I knew, an intelligent, promising child, whilst lying on his death-bed, told his mother that he heard a bird beautifully warbling outside the house, and, apparently in rapture, he listened to the bird's notes. His mother told me this, and she stated further, that she had herself on three different occasions, previously to her elder daughter's death, in the middle of the night, distinctly heard singing of the most lovely kind, coming, as she thought, from the other side of the river, her home being close to a river. She went to the window and opened it, but the singing immediately ceased, and she failed to see anyone on the spot where she had imagined the singing coming from.'

The folklorist J C Davies recorded a variant of this phenomenon which took place near Lledrod, between Tregaron and Aberystwyth in Ceredigion. He wrote: 'One day in the 1850s Mrs Hughes of Cwmllechwedd was standing outside the house when she suddenly heard the sound of singing. She turned around and looked about her, but there was no one to be seen. And yet the maid-servants also heard the singing, so she knew it was not her imagination. Furthermore, she recognised the voice – it belonged to the curate of Lledrod. But where was he? A year later her son, David, only 22 years of age, died. On the day of his funeral, the curate of Lledrod, standing just outside the house, led a hymn, conducting the singing himself, as David's body was being conveyed to the churchyard.'

Somewhat less divine were the portents of a cock crowing at night or the howling of a dog near the house of a dying person. There was nothing ghostly about this behaviour but one does have to wonder what force impelled the animals to behave in this way. A man from Montgomeryshire (now part of Powys), writing in 1874, stated that an old, placid family dog suddenly took to lying outside the door of a room where a relative of the family lay sick. He would then 'set up the most hideous noise any person ever heard'. This was so disturbing that the dog had to be removed from the house. The sick relative died and I'm sorry to have to relate that the dog, a long favourite with the family, was put down afterwards because his weird behaviour had so unnerved the master of the house.

Church spirits

It was formerly believed throughout Wales that a strange, unearthly spirit visited the church at midnight on Hallowe'en and would read out the names of all those doomed to die in the parish over the following twelve months. In the isolated little church of Llangernyw in Conwy this doleful entity was named the 'Angelystor'.

Many people were tempted to hide under the east window of the church and listen out for the grim roll-call but few dared. One could get more than one bargained for! Such was the case of Sion ap Robert, the village wit, who after a few pints on All Hallows' Eve declared the Angelystor a myth and said he'd prove it by visiting the church himself. As the clock struck twelve the overconfident Sion placed his ear against the east window and heard a mournful voice intone 'Sion ap Robert!' The appalled Sion cried out, 'Hold! Hold! I am not quite ready.' His fate was sealed, however, and he died the following year.

A variant of this belief is told from Gwyddelwern, north of Corwen in Denbighshire. Here it was believed that on Hallowe'en night the spirits of all the former church ministers would gather in the churchyard. Particularly courageous (or overly curious) young people would creep into the churchyard in the hope of encountering one of these ghosts, because they were supposed to have the power to reveal to them the names of their future husbands or wives.

Gwrach y Rhibyn

Finally, we must consider this weird spirit. It is the Welsh equivalent of the Irish banshee but even more hideous in appearance. 'Gwrach y Rhibyn' may be translated as 'Hag of the Mountain Drizzle', for her home appears to have been the dreary mists which cling to the high Welsh hills. I can do no better than quote the description of this horrible spirit by the Beddgelert historian D E Jenkins, who uses the word 'goblin', incidentally, in the traditional way of meaning any ghost or other supernatural being:

An early 19th-century illustration of the Irish Banshee. The Welsh equivalent, the Gwrach y Rhibyn, is even more horrible and frightening

'This goblin appeared in the form of a girl of immense size, and of an extremely hideous appearance. She had bright red hair, as coarse as a horse's tail, falling down in rough ringlets over her bony shoulders. Her two cheekbones projected like two ridges, and her curved nose reached almost to her pointed chin. Her eyes flashed red fire from their deep sockets, and when she opened her mouth to give forth her awful howl or shout she showed two or three teeth like the spikes of a harrow, lying the one across the other.

'This she-goblin usually made her appearance on cross-roads or in sharp turnings in the road or path. She came to sight suddenly, just as a bird alights on one's path, and stood in front of the pedestrian with her long bony arms uplifted, and shouted in a cold, shrill voice, "Woe is me! Woe is me!" until one felt his head splitting, his heart and limbs giving way, and his blood running cold in his veins.

'Her appearance invariably foretold some misfortune, and very often the death of the one to whom she appeared; or it might be the death of some near and dear relative. The awful fright which she gave many caused their death or drove them insane, so that it was a common saying when anyone had lost his reason that the old "gwrach" (hag) had bewitched him.'

An account of a meeting with the Gwrach y Rhibyn can be found in an 1831 volume of an old journal, the *Cambrian Quarterly*. It tells of a young ruffian of the name of Owain Fychan, a brawny, hard-drinking fellow, who was making his tipsy way home from an alehouse near Llangollen just after midnight one Hallowe'en. As he entered 'the most frightful part of the road . . . a declivity into a small rugged valley', where the 'the branches of the trees intermingling with and embracing each other over the road made it totally dark', he could just make out ahead of him a female figure. He knew it was a woman because she was wearing a round hat and a blue cloak: 'the usual dress of the female peasantry', as the pre-Victorian writer in the *Cambrian Quarterly* puts it.

Pleased at the notion of some female companionship, Owain tried to catch her up, but somehow the figure always stayed the same distance away from him. She also ignored his loutish attempts to catch her attention. When at length they reached a narrow plank bridge over a stream, Owain finally got his chance. The woman was only halfway across when Owain leapt onto the bridge and familiarly grabbed the woman round her waist. However –

'At that instant the moon shone brilliantly upon them both – the moment he touched her, the hat and cloak had vanished into air – a being – a devil stood in the most threatening attitude before him. Black dishevelled hair, thickly matted and unsightly, fell profusely over a countenance horridly ghastly and disgusting; eyes large, dim, and motionless; cheeks deeply furrowed, and formed of loose flakes, or folds of withered corpse-like skin, the under lip hanging loosely over the chin, and exhibiting long fangs, black as jet, issuing out of colourless gums.'

This horrible spectre let out a bloodcurdling shriek. Then it stooped down to the stream and splashed the water with its skeletal hands, crying out (in Welsh): 'Oh my husband! Oh my husband!' It then floated off the ground and 'lifted up its long lank withered fleshless arms, ready to fold Owain Fychan in its deadly embrace'. This was too much for the usually devil-may-care Owain – he collapsed in a dead faint. When he woke up the following morning, lying in the mud by the stream, he was a changed man. He never more frequented alehouses and his attitude to women was in future considerably more courteous.